How to play
CHESS
and Win!

Tanya Jones

W
FRANKLIN WATTS
LONDON•SYDNEY

First published in 2007
by Franklin Watts

Copyright © Franklin Watts 2007
Franklin Watts
338 Euston Road
London NW1 3BH

Franklin Watts Australia
Level 17/207 Kent Street
Sydney, NSW 2000

Series editor: Jeremy Smith
Designer: Jason Billin
Photography: Steve Shott except where indicated.

Picture Credits: Alamy: 12t, 13t, 18t, 19c. Corbis: 6t, 8t, 10t, 11t, 20t, 22t, 23b, 24t, 26t and c, 27b, 28 all, 29br. istockphoto.com: 4b, 5t, 7r, 11b, 13r, 14t, 16t, 29bl. Shutterstock: OFC.

A CIP catalogue record for this book
is available from the British Library.

Dewey no: 794.1

ISBN: 978 0 7496 7354 3

Printed in China.

Franklin Watts is a division of Hachette Children's Books, an Hachette Livre UK company.

Contents

Why play chess?

For over a thousand years people all over the world have been enjoying the game of chess – its skill, mystery and excitement. Sometimes they have even died for it – usually when they made the mistake of beating a real king!

Playing the game

Chess is a war, and each game is a battle. Some of these battles will be long and drawn-out, some quick and brutal. But the aim is always the same – to trap your opponent's king, so that when you attack him, he has no escape. Each side, Black and White, has an army of 16 soldiers – a king, seven other important pieces and eight pawns. The players take it in turns to move one piece at a time and can attack and capture the other side's pieces, taking them off the board and out of the game. Of course, the fewer pieces you have, the more difficult it is for you to attack your opponent's king, or to defend your own. If your king is attacked and you have no way to protect him, then the game is over, and you have lost. You have been warned…

Endless possibilities

However many times you play, you never know quite how each game will develop. After only five moves, there are trillions of possible positions your pieces could have reached. Imagine how many different positions there could be after 50 moves! And whatever your level, whether you are a beginner or a grandmaster, you can always find opponents who are better, worse or about the same as you.

What do you need to play?

Almost nothing – prisoners and castaways have made chess sets out of soap, stones and silver foil. But it is much easier with a proper board and pieces! There are lots of novelty chess sets in the shops with characters from films, television and history, but these can be very confusing. It is better to use ordinary standard pieces, the kind that professionals use in tournaments. These are called "Staunton" sets after a famous English player of Victorian times called Howard Staunton, the unofficial world champion. If your board is marked with letters and numbers at the edges then this will help you to follow chess notation (explained later in this book).

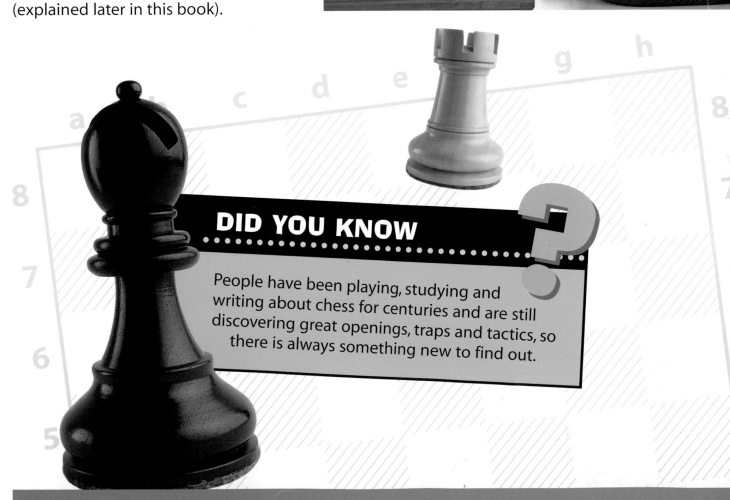

DID YOU KNOW

People have been playing, studying and writing about chess for centuries and are still discovering great openings, traps and tactics, so there is always something new to find out.

How to play – an overview

Each player begins the game with the same pieces on the same squares, and a white square in the right-hand corner in front of him or her ("white on the right"). Pieces capture other pieces by moving onto their square. Pawns are the only pieces which do not capture in the direction in which they move (see pages 8-9).

Ranks and files

On a chess board horizontal rows are called ranks and are numbered from 1 to 8. Vertical columns are called files and are given the letters a to h. Every square has its own name. The white queen begins the game on d1 and the black king on e8. You can set up the pieces with black or white at either end, but chess diagrams always show white at the bottom and black at the top.

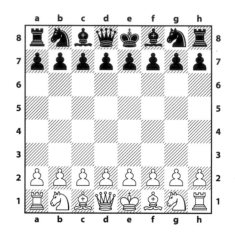

Chess notation

By using abbreviations for the pieces with the names of the squares you can describe any move. For example **Nc3** means that the knight moves to the c3 square. For a pawn move you just need the name of the square the pawn is moving to.

THE PIECES

Name	number on each side	abbreviation	chess symbol
King	1	K	♚
Queen	1	Q	♛
Rook	2	R	♜
Knight	2	N	♞
Bishop	2	B	♝
Pawn	8	none	♟

A very common opening move is **e4,** for example. This means that the white pawn has moved to square **e4**. You can show a capture with an x. For example, Bxd5 means that the bishop has taken the piece that was on the d5 square. If a pawn makes a capture then you need to record which file the pawn came from. For example cxd5.

Who goes first

White always makes the first move, so if two people are playing several games it is fairest to swap colours for each game. The players take it in turns to move. When it is your turn you must move one of your own pieces. You can either move it to an empty square or capture one of your opponent's pieces by moving your piece onto its square. You can record your moves on sheets like the one below. Your aim is to trap your opponent's king – attacking him so that he cannot escape. This is called checkmate and it is the end of the game.

e4

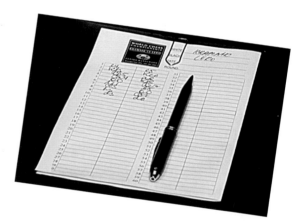

DID YOU KNOW - DRAWS

A draw is declared when:
- Both players agree – usually when their positions are about the same strength.
- When exactly the same position is reached three times.
- The fifty move rule – if there has been no capture or pawn move for fifty moves (not very likely in your exciting games!)
- By perpetual check, insufficient mating material or stalemate – see page 17.

Pawns – the foot soldiers

Pawns are the ones in the front line, the first to go forward and the first to be captured. You have eight pawns at the beginning of the game, and it might seem as though they don't matter very much. But many games are won by the player who ends up with just one more pawn.

The pawn's basic move is one square forwards – it can never move backwards or sideways.

This black pawn can only move to the highlighted square f5.

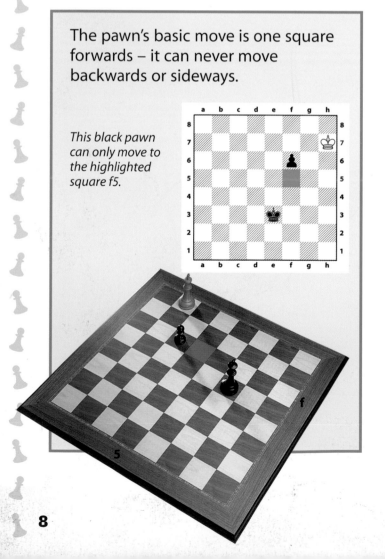

But if the pawn is capturing another chess piece, it can only move diagonally forwards.

*This white pawn can capture the black bishop or the knight but not the pawn, moving to **d6** or **f6.***

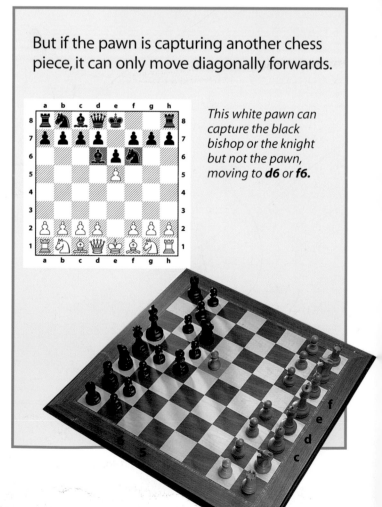

When your pawn is on its starting square it can, if you choose, move two squares forward instead of just one.

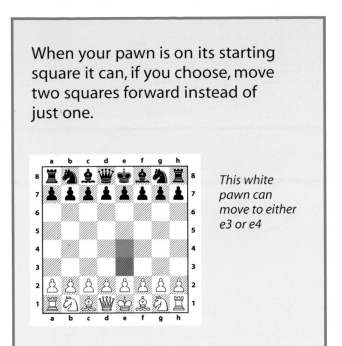

This white pawn can move to either e3 or e4

But beware – you cannot use this two-move rule to avoid being captured by another pawn.

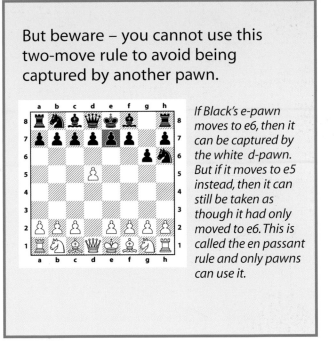

If Black's e-pawn moves to e6, then it can be captured by the white d-pawn. But if it moves to e5 instead, then it can still be taken as though it had only moved to e6. This is called the en passant rule and only pawns can use it.

The pawn's secret weapon

Pawns are always useful – but sometimes they can grow amazingly powerful as well! If you manage to get your pawn all the way to your opponent's back rank (White's back rank is 1 and Black's is 8) then you can **promote** it – turn it into a queen, rook, bishop or knight. (You will almost always choose a queen, as this is the most powerful piece.) It doesn't matter whether or not your original queen is still on the board or whether you have already promoted other pawns – you can end up with two, three or even more queens if you are really lucky!

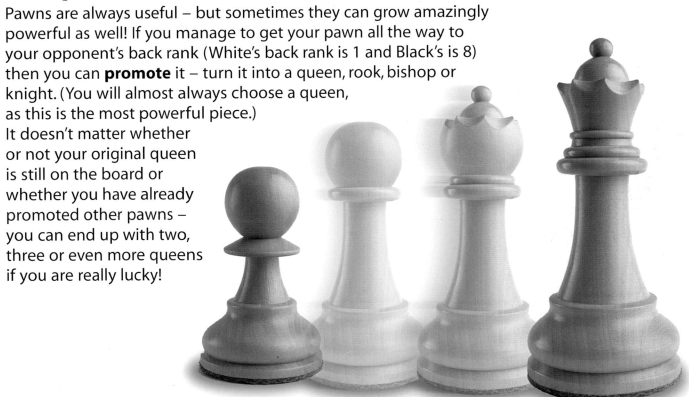

Bishops

Bishops are the pieces with the pointed hats (called mitres in real life), although in French they are called jesters and in German runners.

At an angle

Bishops always move diagonally, as many squares as you like so long as they don't change direction. They can move backwards (still diagonally) but they can't jump.

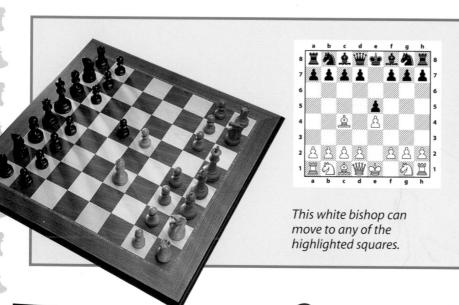

This white bishop can move to any of the highlighted squares.

Two bishops

At the beginning of the game you have two bishops, one on the white or light coloured squares and one on the black or dark ones. Each bishop will always stay on the same coloured squares.

A bishop is usually worth about three pawns, so try not to give it up for less. They are particularly useful in pairs.

TOP TIP

Bishops can be deadly on the **long diagonals** that run between the four corners of the board. A **fianchetto** (Italian for 'little flank') is a move which puts the bishop on to this diagonal, often threatening the opponent's rook.

Knights

The horse's head shaped pieces are called knights (knights used to ride horses, if they could afford them) and each player begins the game with two of them.

The L-shape

The knight's move is peculiar – an L shape made up of two squares in one direction and one at right angles to it (like going around a corner). It can start the move by going forwards, backwards or sideways (not diagonally) but must always complete the same sized L shape.

A jumping piece

The knight has a special power not given to any other chess piece – despite having no legs it can jump! Your knight can jump over your pieces or your opponent's. It doesn't take pieces by jumping over them, only on the square it lands on.

Like the bishop, the knight is worth about three pawns, so bishops and knights are often exchanged – one is captured and then the other. Knights are particularly useful at the beginning of the game as they don't have to wait for pawns to move out of the way.

This black knight can move to any of the marked squares. It can take the pawn on f2.

KEY SKILLS

It is usually a good idea to keep your knights near the centre of the board where they have plenty of spaces to move to – they can get a bit stuck if they are too near the edge.

Rooks

Rooks are often wrongly called castles, but if you want to sound like a professional, remember to use the proper name.

One direction

The rook's move is simple – as many squares as you like in a single direction – forwards, backwards or sideways (but not diagonally, they leave that to the bishops).

This white rook can move to any of the marked squares.

Saving for the endgame

You have two rooks at the beginning of the game and each one is worth about five pawns. Try not to lose your rook for a bishop or knight – these pieces are worth less. They are most useful at the end of the game, especially to give checkmate.

The queen

Each player has only one queen (unless they promote a pawn) but she has more power than any other piece.

Go anywhere!

The Queen can move in a straight line in any direction, including diagonally, but she can't jump or make the knight's L-shaped move.

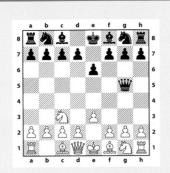

The black queen can move to any of the marked squares.

A powerful weapon

The queen is worth around nine pawns. Always take care of her and treat her with respect – if she is captured it is you who won't be amused.

She's valuable - the Queen.

TOP TIP

Don't bring your queen out too early in the game – she may look threatening but she can easily be trapped.

Here the Black queen has come out early to launch an attack, but now it is White's turn and a White pawn can take the Black queen.

The king

Your king (you only ever have one) is the most important piece on the board, but one of the weakest.

Slow mover

The king can normally only move one square at a time, in any direction, including backwards and diagonally. The only time when the king can move further is during a special move called castling. In this move, you move both your king and rook during the same turn. It is important because it helps bring the rook into the game and make the king secure.

The white king can move to any of the highlighted squares.

Step-by-step: castling kingside

1. Make sure that neither your king nor your kingside rook (the one nearest to it) have already moved, that your king isn't in check and that the bishop and knight have moved out of the way.

Here Black cannot castle because he is in check (see page 16) from White's bishop.

Here Black is in a position where he can begin to castle.

2. Make sure that your king won't move over a square where it would be under attack from an enemy piece. Move your king to the square next to the rook.

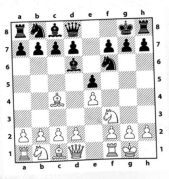

3. Move your rook over the king (this is the one time when a rook can jump). Both the king and rook movements are part of the same move.

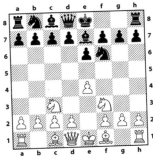

Castling is complete.

Castling queenside

1. When you castle queenside, the king starts off in the position below.

2. Move the king two squares towards the rook on the left. The rook that started on a1 can now hop over the king and land on the next square.

3. Castling complete. The king has moved to c1 and the rook has moved from a1 and to c1.

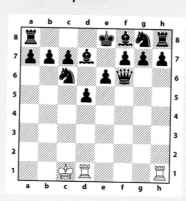

REMEMBER

• You cannot castle if you have already moved your king or the rook that it will castle with.

• You cannot castle if there are any pieces between the king and the rook.

• You cannot castle if your king is in check.

• You cannot castle if your king would pass over a square where it would be in check or if it would be in check at the end of the move.

• The notation for castling kingside is **0-0** and for castling queenside is **0-0-0**.

Check and checkmate

You are **attacking** a piece if you could capture it on your next move.

Check and checking

When a piece attacks the opponent's king, we say that it is giving **check**, or checking, and that the king is in check. If your king is in check then you need to save it immediately – you must not leave it in check and do something else instead, not even check your opponent's king. If you cannot save your king then the game is over and you have lost. This is called **checkmate**.

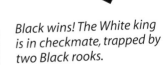

Black wins! The White king is in checkmate, trapped by two Black rooks.

Step-by-step: What to do when you are in check

White is in check from the black queen but can block it by playing his pawn to g3.

1. Don't panic!

2. Think – can you capture the piece that is giving check, using either the king or another piece?

3. Can you block the check with another piece? Of course this will not work if you are in check from a knight, as knights can jump over a blocking piece.

TOP TIP

Remember that you must never move your king into check, or move another piece that leaves your king in check.

4. Can you move your king to a safe square?

Black is in check from White's queen, but can safely move backwards to g8; h8 or f7.

5. If you can do one of these then make your move.

6. If you can't escape from the check then it is checkmate. Smile bravely and suggest another game.

More about drawing

Stalemate happens when one player has no possible legal move. Usually the only piece he can move is his king, but there is nowhere to go except into check.

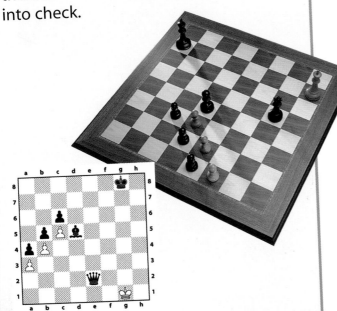

It is White's move. He cannot move any of his pawns, as they are all blocked. He is not in check at the moment, but all the squares around his king are attacked by the black queen or bishop. It is stalemate and the game is a draw.

Perpetual check happens when one player can keep checking the other in every move, but never actually manages to checkmate him. This is a draw because it always leads to the position being repeated three times or to a draw under the fifty-move rule (see page 7).

Insufficient mating material means that neither player has strong enough pieces on the board to checkmate the other. This happens if there are only the kings left, or if neither player has more than his king plus a knight or bishop.

Making you move

The secret of winning chess games is not to make impulsive decisions but to study the board closely and to try to work out what your opponent is planning.

1. Look carefully at your opponent's last move. Is he or she preparing to attack in his next move? What do you think his or her plan is?

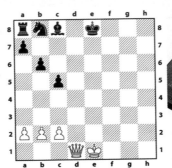

It is Black's move. White is threatening to move his queen to d5 or f3 on the long diagonal. If he can do this then the black rook on a8 will be trapped. If Black sees the threat in time then he can move his bishop to b7, saving the rook.

2. If your king is attacked then you must get out of check on this move. If another of your pieces is being attacked then you have a choice. You could escape from the attack, by moving your piece to a safe square, blocking the attack or capturing the attacking piece. Or instead you could defend your piece. This means moving another piece into position so that if your opponent takes your piece then you can take his in return, or attack another piece of your opponent's of equal or greater value.

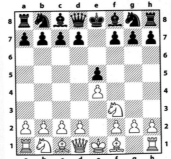

It is Black's second move in the game. White's knight is attacking his pawn on e5. He cannot move the pawn, block the attack or capture the knight. But he can defend the pawn in several different ways. There are seven altogether – can you find them all? (Answer at the bottom of the page).

Answer: Black can play d6 or f6 (pawn moves), Nc6 (moving the knight from b8), Bd6 (moving the bishop from f8), Qe7, Qf6 or Qg5. The best move is probably Nc6 (see pages 20-21 to find out why).

3. Has your opponent left one of his pieces under attack and undefended so that you can take it? (This is called leaving a piece en prise – pronounced "on pree" – with a French accent!) If so, don't be too quick to move. Could it be a trap?

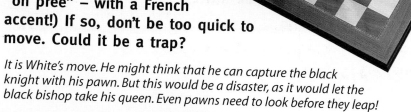

It is White's move. He might think that he can capture the black knight with his pawn. But this would be a disaster, as it would let the black bishop take his queen. Even pawns need to look before they leap!

4. Think about your long-term plan. Where would you like your pieces to be in a few moves' time? Where does your opponent want his pieces to go, and can you stop them? What is the best way to attack his king? Try not to play checking moves just for the sake of it, but only when there is some real purpose – leading to possible checkmate, winning material (enemy pieces) or improving your position.

5. When you are sure what you want to do then make your move carefully. If you are capturing an opponent's piece then remove it from the board without disturbing the other pieces. Then move your own piece to its square.

6. Try not to let your face give away your thoughts – whether you have just seen a winning combination or realised that you are doomed to defeat, your opponent might not see it without a clue from you. And don't trust his expression either – it could all be part of a cunning plan.

ILLEGAL MOVES

If your opponent makes an illegal move, for example moving a pawn backwards or his king into check, then you should point it out and let him change his move. Note: in a tournament or match there may be penalties for making an illegal move.

STRATEGY

Your strategy is your long-term plan – where you want to concentrate your attack and how your pieces will be positioned on the board and work together. Remember that your strategy may have to change as the game develops.

The opening

The beginning of a chess game is called the **opening**. These are often the most important moves you will make, so it is worth taking the time to think carefully.

Open Sesame: secrets of an awesome opening

1. Control the centre of the board – don't waste time by moving pawns at the edge.

2. Develop your pieces – get them into strong and flexible positions. Try not to move a piece more than once in the opening or to block your own pieces.

3. Get your king to safety – usually by castling early.

Step-by-step: how to get off to a good start

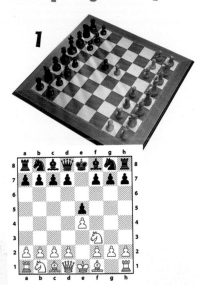

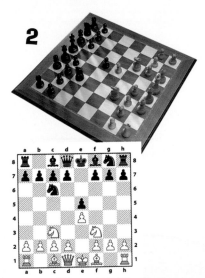

e4 This is always a good opening move for White – opening up a path for the bishop. **E5** Black opens in the same way. **Nf3** A white knight gallops out, attacking the black pawn. It is usually better to develop your knights before your bishops.

Nc6 A black knight ventures forth, defending the black pawn. **Nc3** The other white knight comes out, putting even more pressure on the centre and defending the white pawn.

Nf6 Surprise, surprise – here comes the other black knight. As we predicted, the white pawn on e4 is now attacked, but it's already defended.

Both White and Black now have solid positions that will allow them to bring out their bishops, castle their kings to safety and prepare powerful attacks.

Beware, mate! Opening dangers

Fool's Mate

1. g4 e5 2. f3 Qh4#
The moral of the story is simple – don't move your f and g pawns early in the game.

Scholar's Mate is a nastier
trap, for people who know
which pawns to move first

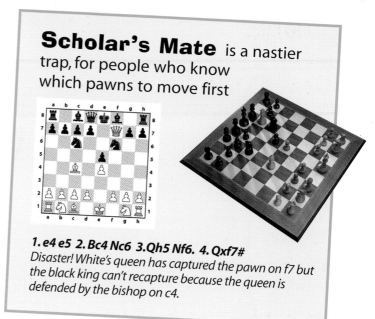

1. e4 e5 2. Bc4 Nc6 3. Qh5 Nf6. 4. Qxf7#
Disaster! White's queen has captured the pawn on f7 but the black king can't recapture because the queen is defended by the bishop on c4.

Avoiding the trap

So what should Black have done to prevent White's queen from taking the pawn?

1. The best move for black would probably have been to move to g6. Placing a pawn here blocks the queen's attack and attacks her at the same time. She is forced to retreat.

2. The white queen might try the attack again, by moving to f3. Again, don't panic! Now the black knight can come out to f6, blocking the attack and developing sensibly.

Tactics

Tactics are clever ways of winning material or even giving checkmate. Usually they work by attacking more than one piece at once, so that the defending player has to give up one to protect the other. Here are a few of the most common and effective chess tactics.

Pins

A pin is an attack on two or more pieces that are in a straight line. The first target is a weaker piece and behind it is a stronger one.

The white bishop is attacking the black knight but if the knight moves then the black king will be in check. The knight is **pinned** to the king, because it cannot legally move away.

The pin above may be annoying to Black but it is not disastrous – he can move his king or let his knight be taken, recapturing the bishop with the king. But sometimes the pin can be a mightier weapon.

The dangers of not castling! It is Black's move. The white rook on e1 is attacking Black's queen on e6. The queen can't move away. The best that Black can do is to capture the rook and let his queen be recaptured by the white queen.

Skewer

A skewer is really just an upside-down pin. It works in exactly the same way, except that it is the stronger piece that is attacked first. This means that the first target has to move away, allowing the second target to be captured.

Here the white bishop is attacking the black queen. When she moves away, the bishop will capture the black rook.

Fork

A fork happens when one piece attacks two or more enemy pieces at the same time. Pawns are good at forking, especially near the beginning of a game.

Black has remembered to begin the game by developing his pieces towards the centre but has overlooked this fork of his bishop and knight. He must give up one of them for only a pawn in return.

TOP TIP

Remember that any piece, and especially a knight, can carry out a fork and that it can be a truly terrifying tactic. Try to get into the habit of looking after your undefended pieces and looking out for chances to fork your opponent.

Endgames

The endgame is the last phase in the chess battle, when most of the pieces have been captured and the flurry of tactics has died down. It is the pawns' moment of glory, as the emptier board makes it easier for them to reach promotion.

A **passed pawn** is one that doesn't have any enemy pawns ahead of it or on either side. It is especially valuable in the endgame, as it is very difficult to stop.

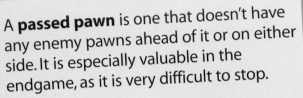

White's a pawn and Black's h pawn are both passed pawns

TOP TIP

Now your king can come out of his refuge to help your own pawns and attack your opponent's. Remember to be very careful, though – checkmates can happen at any time.

NOTATION

To show that a pawn has been promoted, write the pawn move as usual and then, in brackets, the piece that it has been promoted to. For example, **b1(Q)** means that a black pawn has reached the b1 square and become a queen.

Checkmate with two rooks

A pair of rooks in an endgame is a powerful weapon – but you have to know how to use it. Your plan is to trap your opponent's king against any edge of the board so that he can't escape.

1

One rook is on the same rank as the king, giving check while the other one stands guard on the next rank, keeping him from escaping.

2

When the king reaches the edge, the guard rook moves down to check him – and checkmate!

Checkmate with a queen

If you have a queen and a rook then you can checkmate in the same way as with two rooks – but be especially careful to avoid a stalemate. If you have only a queen then she will need the help of your king. Again, you need to begin by driving the enemy king to the edge of the board.

1

2

3

The highlighted squares are controlled by the black queen so that the king must move towards the edge.

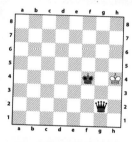

A few moves later, Black has forced White's king to the edge of the board. Now the kings are **in opposition** with just one square between them.

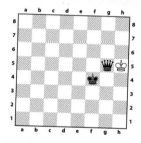

White makes his only possible move, allowing Black's queen to check him from the next square, protected by her king. Checkmate!

TOP TIP

Make sure that you don't leave an undefended rook or queen right next to the king – move across the board if you need more room.

TOP TIP

Remember that you want to trap the king – using the edges of the board, your pieces and his own. You can use a rook or a queen to make a cage for him.

Taking it further

Now that you have mastered the basics of chess, there are lots of ways that you can enjoy improving your skills.

Chess clubs

The most important, of course, is to play plenty of games. Many schools have chess clubs and if yours doesn't, why not suggest it? There are also junior clubs in many towns and cities, and adult clubs which will welcome well-behaved juniors. Contact your national chess federation (see the weblinks on page 31) for more information.

Garry Kasparov, the world number one and most famous figure in chess history.

Internet chess

You can also play chess on the Internet if you have access to a PC. The Internet Chess Club, based in New York, has over 30,000 members, including most of the world's top grandmasters. You can watch their games online or find an opponent nearer your own strength to play a fast "blitz" game. If that sounds a bit daunting, you might prefer to begin at playchess.com which has free chess training and a special beginners' area. Always remember to check with an adult before using the Internet or visiting any new site, and never give out information about yourself online.

THE INTERNET CHESS CLUB
Over 30,000 Members Worldwide

Chess computers

Computers can play chess themselves, of course, as well as hosting human to human games. Specialized chess computers, hand-held or desktop, are still available, and are much more powerful than the ones your mum or dad might have had thirty years ago. But now there are good chess programs for all types of computer, game platform and even mobile phone, so you probably don't need to buy any new hardware.

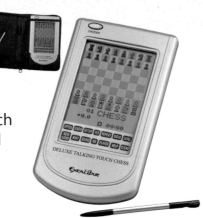

Fritz & Chesster

If you have a PC, or permission to use one, then you have an enormous choice of chess software for practice, training and sheer fun. Avoid the ones that splatter blood across the screen and stick to the programs the professionals use. *Fritz*, from the Chessbase company, is probably the best, and now has a children's version called *Fritz & Chesster*.

Read about it!

Books are the traditional way to learn more about chess, and there are many titles aimed at beginners. Look out for books about openings, tactics, endgames and the famous games of the greatest players. Chess puzzle books are great ways to sharpen up your game. Your local library should have some chess books – but beware of old ones which may use a different, old-fashioned notation. There are also several chess magazines with articles, puzzles and information about forthcoming tournaments.

DVDs

Or if you'd prefer to be in front of the TV than curled up with a book, there is a wide range of chess DVDs now available. These can teach you about different openings, help you to improve your general game or let you relax and be inspired as you watch the rapidplay games of the world's greatest grandmasters.

Playing in a tournament

One of the best ways to try out your new skills and make friends is at a chess tournament. Tournaments, or "congresses", are held every weekend and during school holidays right across the country.

How to enter a tournament

1. Make sure you have met all the requirements – sometimes you need to register in advance or be a member of your national federation. There will usually be sections for players of different ages or strengths. Telephone or email the organizers if you are not sure – they will be pleased to welcome a newcomer.

2. Before each round of the tournament, a pairing list will be put up, showing which board you will play at, who your opponent will be and whether you will be White or Black. Make sure you have a pen and, if possible, something to drink.

Pairing List

1. Smith, Jamie   Jones, Claire
2. Brown, Emily   Evans, Josh

If you are Claire Jones, then you will be playing against Jamie Smith on Board 1 (the "top board". He will be White and you will be Black (White's name is always given first).

3. Give yourself plenty of time to find your board and write your name and your opponent's at the top of your scoresheet. Shake hands with your opponent at the beginning of the game.

4. In a tournament, once you have touched a piece you must move it, so think very carefully before you make your move – you cannot take it back. If a piece is not properly on its square then say "*j'adoube*" (French for "I adjust") before you put it right – then you will not have to move it.

5. Nearly all tournaments use a chess clock – a double clock showing how much time each player has left. You have a certain amount of time for all your moves, and if you run out of time then you usually lose the game. When you have made your move, press the top of your clock. This will stop your clock from ticking and start your opponent's.

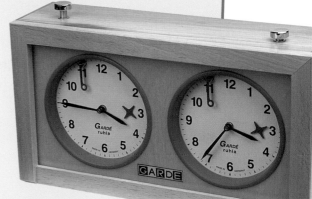

6. In most tournaments you will need to write down your moves on your scoresheet. You can do this just before you move or after pressing your clock. Write down your opponent's move as soon as he or she has played it.

7. If you have any problems during the game, put up your hand and an arbiter (chess referee) will come over and help you. He or she won't tell you which move to play, though!

8. At the end of the game, shake hands again and mark the result on your scoresheet. Then take your scoresheet or results slip to the organizers. If there is time, ask your opponent if he or she would like to analyse (look through) your game in a special room or area where you can talk. This is a really good way to improve your chess.

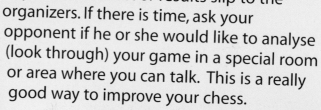

Glossary

Analysis
Looking at the moves of a game after it has finished.

Back rank checkmate
Checkmate on the 1st or 8th rank.

Capture
Move where one piece takes another.

Castling
A special move allowing the king to move over a rook.

Check
Attack on the king.

Checkmate
Attack on the king that he cannot escape from.

Develop
To move your pieces from their starting squares into good positions.

Discovered check
A piece moves out of the way, allowing another piece to give check.

Draw
Game where neither player has won or lost.

Draw by repetition
Draw where the position is repeated three times.

Endgame
The last phase of a chess game when there are few pieces left on the board.

En passant rule
Rule allowing a pawn to take an opposing pawn that has moved two squares.

En prise
Where a piece is attacked and not defended.

Fianchetto
A move putting a bishop on to a long diagonal.

Fifty-move rule
Draw with no captures or pawn moves for 50 moves.

File
Vertical column on a chess board – marked a to h.

Fool's Mate
Checkmate allowed by moving the f and g pawns.

Fork
Attack on two pieces at the same time.

Grandmaster
The highest level of chess player.

Illegal move
A move not allowed in the rules of chess such as putting your king into check.

International Master
The second highest level of chess player.

J'adoube / "I adjust"
Statement to show that player does not intend to move the piece that he is touching.

Long diagonal
One of the diagonal rows of squares that run between the corners of the board.

Notation
Short way of describing squares and moves.

Opposition
Position where two kings stand opposite one another.

Passed pawn
A pawn with no enemy pawns ahead on the same or next files.

Perpetual check
One player checks the other on every move, leading to a draw.

Pin
Attack on two pieces in a line with the weaker piece attacked first.

Promotion
Rule allowing a pawn to become a piece when it reaches the opponent's back rank.

Rank
Horizontal row on the chess board – numbered 1 to 8.

Rapid play
Fast chess game with each player given around 30 minutes to make all his moves.

Rating / grade
Number showing the strength of a chess player - the higher the better.

Resign
To give up the game.

Scholar's Mate
Quick checkmate by double attack on f2 or f7.

Scoresheet
Form for player to write down his moves.

Skewer
Attack on two pieces in a line with the stronger piece attacked first.

Stalemate
Draw because one player has no legal move.

Strategy
Long-term plan for winning a game.

Tactics
Ways of winning pieces or giving checkmate.

Touch-move rule
The rule that if a player touches a piece he must move it (or take it if it is his opponent's).

Tournament / Congress
Chess competition with several rounds.

Weblinks

Chess Federations
www.fide.com World Chess Federation
www.bcf.org.uk English Chess Federation
www.chessscotland.com Chess Scotland
www.welshchessunion.co.uk Welsh Chess Union
www.icu.ie Irish Chess Union

Online chess playing sites
www.chessclub.com Internet Chess Club
www.playchess.com

Chess software
www.chessbase.com Chessbase, publishers of Fritz

Suppliers of chess equipment, books etc.
www.chess.co.uk
London Chess Centre
www.bcmchess.co.uk/shop.html BCM Chess Shop

Chess magazines
www.bcmchess.co.uk
British Chess Magazine
www.chess.co.uk
Chess Monthly
www.newinchess.com
New In Chess magazine
www.chesscafe.com
Online articles and reviews

Note to parents and teachers: Every effort has been made by the Publishers to ensure that these websites are suitable for children, that they are of the highest educational value, and that they contain no inappropriate or offensive material. However, because of the nature of the Internet, it is impossible to guarantee that the contents of these sites will not be altered. We strongly advise that Internet access is supervised by a responsible adult.

Index